Allegro

(Composed 1762 at the age of 6)

W. A. MOZART
arranged by Leon Block

Wiegenlied*
Song

W. A. MOZART
arranged by Leon Block

Andante

Schla-fe, mein Prin-zchen, schlaf ein, es ruhn nun Schäf-chen

und Vö- ge - lein, Gar- ten und Wie - se ver -stummt,

auch nicht ein Bien-chen mehr summt,

Lu - na mit sil - ber-nem Schein gu-cket zum Fen-ster her-

ein, schla - fe beim sil - ber -nen Schein,

schla -fe, mein Prin-zchen, schlaf ein, schlaf

ein, schlaf - ein!

* attributed to Bernhard Flies

Canzonetta

from "Don Giovanni"

W. A. MOZART
arranged by Leon Block

The Abduction from the Seraglio
from the Overture

W. A. MOZART
arranged by Leon Block

Die Kleine Spinnerin

Song

W. A. MOZART
arranged by Leon Block

Theme (Romanza Pedrilla)

from "The Abduction from the Seraglio"

W. A. MOZART
arranged by Leon Block

Theme

from Sonata in E minor for Violin and Piano

W. A. MOZART
arranged by Leon Block

Tempo di Minuetto

Aria "Il Mio Tesoro"

from "Don Giovanni"

W. A. MOZART
arranged by Leon Block

Il mio te - so - ro in - tan - to, an - da - te, an - da - te, a con - so - lar, e del bel ci - gli il pian - to cer - ca - te dia - sciu - gar cer - ca - te, cer - ca - te, cer - ca - te, dia - sciu - gar, cer - ca - te dia - sciu - gar!

Eine Kleine Nachtmusik

Theme from 1st movement

W. A. MOZART
arranged by Leon Block

Eine Kleine Nachtmusik

Theme from 2nd movement
(Romance)

W. A. MOZART
arranged by Leon Block

Alla Turca

from Sonata in A major for Piano

W. A. MOZART
arranged by Leon Block

Theme

from Piano Sonata No. 1 in C

W. A. MOZART
arranged by Leon Block

Theme

from Rondo in D major for Piano

W. A. MOZART
arranged by Leon Block

Theme

from Piano Concerto No. 21, 2nd movement

W. A. MOZART
arranged by Leon Block